LETTERS & BUILDINGS

LETTERS & BUILDINGS.

SUBITO PRESS 2014

ISBN: 978-0-9831150-9-0

Design & typesetting by HR Hegnauer | www.hrhegnauer.com
Text typeset in Adobe Garamond Pro.

Subito Press
Department of English
University of Colorado at Boulder
226 UCB
Boulder, CO 80309-0226
subitopress.org

Distributed by Small Press Distribution
1341 Seventh Street
Berkeley, California 94710
spdbooks.org

Generous funding for this publication has been provided by the Creative
Writing Program in the Department of English and the Innovative Seed
Grant Program at the University of Colorado at Boulder.

If one should sit down in a room
before a glass window, she could
if she looked out of one eye only
keeping her head still, trace upon
the intuition. A perspective projection
of past houses or other objects once
known, outside, to be hers and lost
by time, by making all the lines of her
perspective coincide with real lines
outside: in other words, each point
bears relation to an indestructible
vestige of how we felt when we said
"how" or "notwithstanding." The glass
part of a straight line drawn from
the corresponding part of the real
object to the pupil of the eye, forms
a bridge to the empirical self. Having
made the trace, she would find that every
sphere of sense, every intermittent
stimulus, if she moved her head ever
so little, no longer fit over real things.
The picture surface need not be
between the observer and the objects
to be drawn, but in taking on the habit
of the one, will necessarily distort
the make and matters of the other.

1.

One day you finish to be a boy.

The protogenesis of form is a character of compromise.

Slight of eachness
other: grief long kept
edged behind ideal

lies: our not-willing, non-
cause (I am) not
known to know if

The eye travels paths cut out for it in work.

What left to misinterpret: nothing else
outside effects of isolation once embraced
as growth abatement, a lone reflexive way

to circumscribe involvement and existence and
one stunted satisfaction limitation shaped
into condition, excitation, self-aphasic

efforts to reject rejection and dehumanize the
voice, emotive purpose, to adduce within
the hearing thoughts in air a knowledge

that the shape a body takes approximates
the distance from itself to its own end
within its subdivision of the once-together air into

a preference for a deafness to the noises
other people offer and a begging out for anyone
to need me. Put domestic: every year a house

within a house its home and I between the two
a crawlway lost the what in want went
wrong. The primary figure is repeated

without end; permanence waves a hand
when it is pause and blame and listen to the vagueness
that that vagueness forms around him, his

made sad with explanation. Layered in the everything
ambiguous relying on resemblance to repair
the beauty of the blandnesses that stand in

our nothing much writ large. It (the sadness) keeps
expanding into objects which in overlap evince
a humanness of faults, reacting to insistence

that by adding just a color—what it means is all
the physiologies of thingness we latch onto—we can
elementally enhance it, reveal its meaning

gleaned from pasts demanded spoken in the "here
then" and "me too" and "if she," rather than accept we are
conditioned to deny within our so-called drives

there is a silence too impossible to flee.
Nothing can be said which isn't true.
The fever of duration is an endlessness

our loss caused as it faltered absolutely
inexhausted. And any voice one hears is there, between
the nearest waters where its seen and all the water

farther with reflection, and, within it, doubtful space
when one trains the eye for near or far.
A cautionary surface, a confusion of the purpose

outside of his own noise, an other other with no rest
reflex; another body at a distance so slight
it is impossible to distinguish what in want

resembles each and, as it is, is an actualization
the intersection of desire and appearance made, or
a deletion of its two distinct perspectives.

Another trap presents itself: the background
can't be hidden. Because it rests on nothing.
Because it is the all else all else rests upon.

A new red door on that same old house
still opens on that house, still holds the evident and the
awkwardness at the mistrust which says this was

the inevitable conclusion, that we're better off now
anyhow. All the while that hand keeps waving back
redactions of adaptability in form, clear and inward

variations. Position deviation. All the various
elements of a picture, split and combined, reveal
a substance, knowing contrast, and at the same time

reciprocity of sight; a way to be alone
up on the wall. We call it our accesion and adopt
distortion as our own: how speaking need debilitates

the language of a want. The languages of want
deaf to all the disparate voices. Here then is a
brick-shaped body, just at the edge of the water.

A distance of psychosomatic withdrawal.

Two straightpins cluttering
up the nothing;

the laughter, white ambush;

wrests the risen sickness.

Proportion is a correspondence among the measures

according to, is merged in other
feelings; her light either. He too felt his

eye is a disease of on what grounds
a formless gift in black—in addition

other's sympathy—or answered by.
Aviation (concept); warmly motile

contents, connectioned. Soon as wills
want to reproduce, encompass

in her, he with else another
feeling so conveys: the hand lacks

the foot similar, hand to affect
illness. Company to cause the victim

intermediate and medial treatment
saves two reasons all diseases

the average of spherical bodies
yields upon a surface unreliable

pictures of their bodies coalescing—
a false symmetric body of the bodies—into

lifelike deprivation. Circular as the set is
to its surface, there they curve

among straight lines to frame relation
preternatural, is and will

commensuration's unremarkable
effects on secant surface, which is cut.

While within the body, it informs
and, formed, is bound for when dependent

eachnesses: relational disharmony or
naming synesthetic obligation

as its light in, other feelings
want, he too felt. That one eye.

Morbid in the sympathy
with another pliability of dark air

in answer, the association of nerve
divides divides. One disorder

reproduced, as in by therefore with its
feeling, of another it contained

believed complete, thus duplicated.
Required sufficiently, affected

sufficiently; the company of
disease increased together makes

performed the medial treatment
for the victims of two reasons

but if you doubt that in us our
movements follow paths of perfect

isolation, I answer you my
nearly meant gesture. Why are your

real movements this. A nameless touch
we followed falsely on along an every

dwelling flight path, a projection
without patience and on spirals. You speak your

friction or divisive or continually
movements, and the you which speaks you

something is just another thought
shaped into an passage where

the error does not lead—its in for nothing
gives, courses through courses

together has her light or he felt.
The fact that lapse answers back

whose eye in lack is too much felt
delusion, ables rest inside the sympathy

a difference flexibility. Association
touched a nerve which is warned

with the thing one refreshed together
wants: a disjunction of disorder

where inside her wants to be like that
with him. To include and perform

enough effect that one receives
enough to out deficient company

enough the victim all diseases
with the company of a treatment.

That virtues acquired by death have retroactive effects.

Untogether; overnatural

disarticulation any natural

movement makes of

things should not be

broken. Seeing sky

the mouth insides sky

Once when hours, once when it is over

to find out. Its picture's
frame, walls all

long since the paper lost
off. A someone's

house without your
left of your voice to call

onto, a close unlevel floor
the course toward without which our

approach closed over
whole. Lasting. I have

two hearts, kept covered—
one too much. The fixture

held too far close goes
still half, slow growth.

And, not content with circumscription, spreads.

Though I may not ever recognize the places
I have seen it, it is still an ornament, an ornament
known well; I know its name, I traced
those lines, and feel easy now about it. It looks

like this, though I don't mean that, I mean it's something
like that but with dimension, despite the way
I choose to draw it. A picture made of words
rejecting anything always shown to me. I do no

interpreting. And again, once more, allegiances
to structures dominate the field of structures and, again, less
rewarding spontaneities reign. A certain trend
toward rigidity predominates; asymmetrical

ornamentation, held as the naturally occurring
opposition to precision representation, ignores
altogether coherent rhythms. The movement to erase
whatever overlap exists between how we think

when we act and how we talk about it rests
in the shapes that I see I want to say are not
simply shapes; one shape seen is only ever all the shapes
I know; it is a shape marked in advance, a shape

I patterned in me, and because it corresponds
to such a self-pattern is it this familiar shape
methodized and represented in a group
of spatial objects; close, known, irregularly solid

solids, symmetrically figured; each, then, takes a shape
that elaborates in rearrangement its impression
on me, because it is the preperformance of a body
I am familiar with, because there are solution

lists and this, this bodied, is on one such list
because it represents a kind of object I am
familiar with. Because it gives an instantaneous
impression of relation, varied associations

carried in connection with it, I know what it is
called, I know I have seen it, and I know what it is
used for, and because I seem to be familiar
with it, a name occurs to me as its name and I tell

myself: of course. It represents, and may again, a face
familiar, recognized, in and of itself a face
I know and I, knowing, recognize the features seen
though I may not ever recognize its place.

A noticeable instance of transition.

Hasn't the moving, the
recentness, left

severe need now.
You reason why it happened

why land all around
ills. Has to. Un-

deduced reply, never
halves, perceived

the likewise none
believing. Gesture hides the

message, this
awkward near likeness.

Into it the way a
luck recurs, left these

behind: detachment, "it
isn't." Miserable

loyalty, I am prepared
at any given

moment to continue
this without you.

Saying it, as it
was, too close to distant

pleasure, led it first to
you and left you.

2.

Conversation in black laughs;
Or, This is the way we ride the bike.

every point of sight is a cause
placed directly opposite
the body; the limits

                                    bodied are the vanishing
                                    landscapes of personal ill.

                         And points of picture hurt the center.
                              And pursuit itself enjoys him.

The secondary cause of all things:

An assessment is necessary to determine whether fathers
have attachment disorders

to be without conviction.

Circle the items if they are frequently, or sometimes, true.

Father can't keep friends for an age-
appropriate length of time.

It is in
this way—in

order to
master personal

attentiveness—we
resort to, speak

from, believe
with our most

elegant yet
obsolete needs.

He never nears the saying, expected less to listen.

How do I [   ] on the life of my father.

Men today revealed in an utterance so bland.

Father doesn't do as well in life as father could.

Father pretends things aren't really problems when caught

doing something wrong.

The limit of the body helps the runner.

                                        Disfolding, winds not
                                        uninfluenced. Only

                                        our most committed
                                        theories of relation

                                        could explain, or hope
                                        to enjoy, any given

                                        point since; the
                                        pauses unmistakable.

How do I [   ] in the life of my [   ].

                              A home of homes in performance
of home;

the death of expectation.

Father ________ the passage of time, often ________ or silly things.

Father's hypervigilance: .

)

)

)

My father does not know or does not care that my father may be hurt.

                                  A strong light like sunlight.

My father plays with sharps, elopes; my father seems oblivious to the
fact my father may be hurt.

                    Father deliberately ruins (his) things or other's things

                                                    What is the
                                                    why we have
                                                    it less then

Vulgarity exists
because it rests

on nothing. Hands move to communicate and the

                                        to stop doing what my father
                                                    wants to do.

unbelievable reasons for how my father got these things.

How do I [   ] from the [   ] of [   ].

What we found to make it

stand was to accept the very notion of future.

Paintings: we arbitrarily cut away
different parts until nothing is left.
Not only the distance from the eye
but also the slope of our floor line.

The perpetual aggression of the unforeseen.

My father hoards, sneaks food, unusually eats (eats paper, raw sugar,
non-foods, package mixes, baker's chocolate, etc.).

Often does not make eye contact when adults want to make eye contact.

Then we began to fix the distance
from the eye to our picture.

We think you might by now alone
perform the functions of machines.

Find the lower lefthand corner.

New positions of the points now

that the page is torn out:

       between the
       very near

       water where
       you see it

       farther water
       sight reflected

       there then is
       the neutral of

       ideal you see
       refracted thought

       not things not
       limned by

       thought past
       with dry eyes

A doubtful space where you
train the eye for near or far.

_______________________________ :: I give you this ring as a visible and
constant symbol of my promise to be with you.

My father doesn't seem to learn from his mistakes or from a consequence (he continues the behavior despite the punishment).

Meaning: he could say that ever since he heard waves begin again once more in bright air, remembrances of boyhood, brown wasps, and broken vessels have all become the error and the future of bright air, and that the life of a wave is not once more to the lake, but a stranger in the periodic table.

Meaning: permanence narrows as though by sunlight or beginnings.

How do I [   ] on the [   ] of [   ].

Father chatters. Mutters. Repeated questions make no sense.
He is hard to understand when talking.

How do I [   ] from the life of my [   ].

Does he seem preoccupied by how you (or other children, child
strangers) are doing? Why do you think he does this? Do you ever
think it too much for a man his age?

And, again, again.
A general theory of vanishing points.

The nature of a building, even if it
fails, is to remind us of our fragility:

the longer contact of letters and relapse.

The surface whispers:

later on you will try
your hand at accident.

                              (It is not the outbreak of specificity
which eludes the irreparable: there are vaguer but more troublesome
warnings to signify our way up through the water.)

How do I [   ] before the life of my father.

the eye insinuates:

                                        I know of no prettier
                                        problem in perspective
                                        than excommunication
                                        from the temporal.

                              (Difference: if the light went out
the other way, the ray up through waters would be a simple
plan with an empty they.)

Reflected on the glass,

which one, analyzed, escapes its
simple box with a ground plan?

the surface of the glass need
not even be plane.

We're talking with children about their fathers and some of the
things they do. So we can hope to understand your father better.

Let him imagine
a picture story in schematic
pictures, thus more

                                    akin to language
                                 narratives than pictures.
                                 Sentences in a word-

Is he one to sit where he is and wait for you (or other children, child
strangers), or does he come and tell you when he's hurt?

                                 language approximate
                                 a picture in this picture-
                                 language much more closely

Does he cry or cling to you, or is he simply wary? cautious?

                                 than he thinks. In water.
                                 Reflections in calm water.
                                 Schematic waves of

Take turns talking and gesturing with you?

simple construction form
reflections which, reflections
being limits of real

Does he seem to be afraid of you?
Or to do exactly what you want, in sorts of automatic ways?

waveforms and always
close to them, remain
sufficient guides for

Ever more shy or less shy than now?

pictorial purpose. Remember:
he doesn't have to translate
pictures to understand

Often wander without purpose?

                              them, any more than he
                              translates photographs or
                                      films into color

Does he approach you accidentally, as in pursuit of a rolling toy?

                              pictures—suppose he said:
                              "Something is a picture
                              only in a picture language?"

          [   ]

What it is between us and the sun;

a picture of two persons, overwhelmed with pity.

The angle of reflection equals angled obsolescence.
The perpetual aggression of misunreadiness.

reflections in water. Reflections in calm water.

To avoid this, a new device presents itself:

My does not seem to feel guilt. Does not seem to feel rage. My does not seem to feel need. My does not thank or feel thanks. Expression unclear. Doesn't wait for me to come to him. A touch won't sway. He shows no interest in engagement. New things do not attract him. He spills and smears on himself and on floors all the time. He isn't angry at me unless I ask (or he is very tired). No interest in such contact. He is sometimes lost or slow to understand what I want. Can take such things or leave them. Having none at all. Often asks me for help. Too often asks me for help. Doesn't grow fond of people easily. Doesn't want a lot of contact. Happy moods are very changeable. He is cautious, fearful. Everything a difficulty. Is skilled with objects, pencils. Even if he warms to visitors, he runs to me with fret and cry. My does not share with new adults when he is asked. Bumps, drops, or stumbles happen throughout the day. He neither likes nor dislikes music. Not especially eager. Mine is slow to adjust to people or things. I am the only one he allows to comfort him.

As the surface of water approaches, reflection lessens and the second voice just stops.

There is a text which can make us admit anything in this world, but it is not powerful enough to make us admit the world itself.

It was in a clinic waiting room.

We cut away the different parts
until nothing was left but what we found

                              necessary to make it stand.

        Here then is a [   ] at the [   ] of [   ].

the search ends in desertion:

the halved elapse of letters and buildings:

the simple plan of an empty they

                                        in pursuit of a rolling toy.

3.

Point and Line to Plane.

Was suddenly finished. It was as simple as that. As
long as the child's walking is imperfect, he tends
to walk and walk, often with no other goal than
walking. And in being granted understanding and
realization—not in words and sequential thoughts,
but in the sudden bliss of internal illumination—he   *Force from without.*
is already free, liberated from all natural artificial
bonds and barriers. Continuity can be arranged
from any place. And so. Let us regard a particle of
water which moves within a constant stream through
a narrow tube. What if we said we had done this
thing? Everything here depends upon proportions, as
everything previous—the absolute is reduced by the
relative, the pronounced by subdued sound. It's all
in the valuing. A judgment on judgment. We could
say: It is a phenomenon that there are people who
can't learn this or that. Even though on the surface
the individual appearances of plants differ so greatly
from each other that their inner relationship remains
obscured—even though these phenomena seem
chaotic to the superficial eye—they can, nevertheless,
on the basis of their common inner necessity, be
traced back to the same root.

There used to be a wall here, now we have gates,
hence the curve of the street.

Whatever things are plastic to his hands, those things
he must remodel into shapes of his own, and the
result of the remodeling, however useless it may be,
gives him more pleasure than the original thing. Light
outside equals realness in the opening.

It was warm and quiet.

But there is still a great difference between the two
forms of procedure: between the usual description
and enumeration of separate disturbances, such
as those of visual or linguistic performances, and
our procedure, which is primarily directed toward
the cognition of the whole, and, within this frame
of reference, seeks to analyze as many individual
performances as possible. This is not awareness but
a name of it. It can come like the fog, in silence
and almost without his knowing, for then it will
not come forthrightly as a form of memory but as
something else, as a pure and particularized desire,
a direct and focused appetite. These symbols are so
general that they even precede the differentiation
into letters and numerals and can be named at
will. Artifacts require care. We may regard this
methodological principle as a general postulate.
Making it impossible to see out. Taking possible from
proven. For events are what they were, and what
follows is how I understood them then.

A view which is stagnant. If our wills are
indeterminate, so must our beliefs be, etc. In this
respect, music is not innocent. Everywhere codes
analyze, mark, restrain, train, repress, and channel
the primitive sounds of language, of the body, of   *Inner parallels.*
tools, of objects, of the relations to self and others.
A beautiful and seductive head, a woman's head, I
mean, makes one dream, but in a confused fashion,
at once of pleasure and of sadness; conveys an

idea of melancholy, of lassitude, even of satiety—a
contradictory impression, of an ardor, that is to
say, and a desire for life together with a bitterness
which flows back upon them as if from a sense
of deprivation and hopelessness. I am unable to
comprehend how a person of substance could take a
newspaper in her hand without a shudder of disgust.
The simplest thing is the most incredible thing, the
most incredible thing is the most remarkable thing,
which requires examination. It seems as if the path
is lined with books, with the thoughts of others that
share only the agreement to disagree, to be mutually
exclusive as if ideas had a materiality that simply
made it unthinkable for two or more to co-exist in the
same moment without displacing each other.

At least that's how I felt on colder nights. If the
movement of thought, the renewal of circumstance,
was conveyed through kinetics, then the street would
ripple as if it were reflected in water, and the earth
would shake underneath the water.

It's the signification of real sensations that the *Above and below.*
mundane fights against. Several standing trees were
already withered, others were fading, and next
to them were some that were still quite fresh and
without presentiment of the approaching fire that was
menacing their roots. The same holds true for those
who emphasize the primacy of bodily phenomena.

Health or sickness—that is the difference. In
performances of the normal organism, the total

organism forms the background against which the
figure process, taking place in a circumscribed area,
stands out. It's the same scenario played out over
eons. Soft targets. It appears as if all our concrete
manifestations of selfishness might be the conclusions
of as many syllogisms, each with this principle as
the subject of its major premise, thus: Whatever is
me is precious; this is me; therefore this is precious;
whatever is mine must not fail; this is mine; therefore
this must not fail, etc. It appears as if this principle
inoculated all it touched with its own intimate quality
of worth; as if, previous to the touching, everything
might be a matter of indifference, and nothing
interesting in its own right; as if my regard for my
own body were an interest not simply in this body,
but in this body only so far as it is mine. He feels a
firm conviction that neither a hostile element nor a
malevolent spirit will be able to hinder him from
assuming a transfigured form in which to partake of
immeasurable bliss in direct contact with the divinity
from which it emanates. You can be our referee.
Toward what are drives driving? If the gradual loss of
my memory, properly understood as grace, served to
make my life gradually more meaningful to me, how
could I call it a dysfunction?

It was exactly the same as that day in the landscape
room. They were telling how in the mountains,
when the wild apples would ripen and fall into the
streams, the streams would overflow. The fact is that
discontinuity comes in if a new nature comes in at
all. There is, in the act of love, a great resemblance

to torture or to a surgical operation. None of this
makes sense. There are so many things one would be
wiser about. Where indecision is great, as before a
dangerous leap, consciousness is agonizingly intense.
I had days of which to be proud.

I was back at the old business of setting up the
proper rites, sacraments and artifacts, and the effects
on my spirit were immediately felt by me and
manifested to everyone, so that no longer was there
any demeaning confusion of how I should relate
my divided self to the distinct, contrasting realities
around me, for no longer was there any contrast
between them, or them and me.

The question then arises: Do we need this gap in
time intact?

In brief, I lost my bearings, my senses failed, and when
I recovered from my unconsciousness and fright, I
found myself at the foot of a linden tree, having been
thrown against it by the swiftly rising fence.

*Single sound as
composition.*

That is what relationship tends toward. Equivalent
montage. An exchange between bodies—through
work, not through objects. Work being substance,
regardless of origin; any gift. Any noise, when two
people decide to invest their imagination and their
desire in it, becomes a potential relationship, future
order. I intend to hold that principle sacred to the end
of my days, although now and then one may entertain
doubts when confronted with people who apparently

have better success without such principles. I suppose
I'm talking about something vague.

Nearly our whole lives are employed in foolish
inquiries. Insects that have no stomachs persistently
eat; withered ferns bloom again and reflower; absent
members grow again.

A work no one except the composer can perform,
often for lack of instruments specially invented for it.

She sees the world, but it appears to her estranged,
as if disconnected from her past and the present
moment. But there comes a moment when the hope
of relatives is somehow artificial and dishonest. We
don't know the points of intersection where we can
or cannot trust our own thoughts. Where before *False ways.*
there was a whole, a unity, there are suddenly two
separated pieces, two distinct cells, and then where
there were two, there are suddenly four, then eight,
and so on, as the man stumbles through blocks of
time, dividing and subdividing like an amoeba drifting
through a pool of stagnant water. Families stay
together. No matter how we may define normality
there are certainly many digressions from the
norm that do not mean being sick. Centuries don't
disappear. They don't decay. I strode down the path
of least resistance, as it were, by simply refusing to
acknowledge this lustful seizure and the seizures that
regularly every afternoon followed it, like links in a
binding chain, as being anything more than some
natural expression of my body, no less natural than

the continued growth of the hair of my head or
the hair of my beard or the nails of my fingers and
toes. All our pleasure in life depends on the regular
occurrence of external things. Having said all that,
it must appear unusually difficult to gain the correct
attitude for our dealings with anomalies in the sense
of deviation from an average, or, even more so, from
an ideal type. The situation is somewhat different
if we regard anomaly from the point of view of the
individual norm.

But nothing would take shape for me: I lacked an
event, a plot, in which to incorporate these things.
Cattle do not help a wounded comrade; on the
contrary, they are more likely to dispatch him.

The long day. I acted as I believed I had to act. What
harshness and clamor existed before now faded into
the sound of the waves unfolding themselves onto
the flattened shore. The matter does not end with
them. Our higher aesthetic, moral, and intellectual
life seems made up of affections of this collateral and
incidental sort, which have entered the mind by the
back stairs, as it were, or rather have not entered the
mind at all, but got surreptitiously born in the house.
Whether acquired ancestral habits played any part at
all in their production was still an open question in
which it would be as rash to affirm as to deny. But I
hear them.

Do not misunderstand me: controlling noise is not
the same as imposing silence in the usual sense. And

that is perhaps the key to the process of repetition
as it is taking root today. An infinite in little. It is
already present—in its fragility and instability, in its
transcendence and fortuitousness, in its requirement
of tolerance and autonomy, in its estrangement from
the commodity and materiability—implicit in our
everyday relation to music. If the present is conceived
of as part of the eternal present, then what follows is
the exact coincidence of the part and the whole. But
consciousness is prerequisite in order for productivity
to find its manifestation. Continuity can be arranged
from any place. It is the multitude of methods of
correlation that reveals the purpose of life. Today, for
instance, the heart has lost much of its predominance
as compared to the capillaries. They opened their
umbrellas and stepped out from under awnings for
a stroll. The isolated part of the system has a limited
environment. The confession is recounted in detail.
A roll of thunder is heard. Phones ring. This is how
plot travels through time! So why should I now, both
confronted and aware, not pick an act and act, hear
a noise and isolate, choose a single strand and pursue
it to its source. What I see is what I hear and there is
still a flattened shore.

I'll repeat—

Silence. Anything new there? Because life is like
that. Ordered behavior and preferred behavior. A
descriptive catalogue and undefined terms. Straight
lines which have two points, planes which have three
points, parallels to a given line which have one point,

in common, coalesce throughout.

Here a slight misunderstanding arose, for we were as
yet unused to each other's company and our respective
ways of expressing ourselves. A hidden harmony is
better than a visible. The deadness that is at stake   *Above and below.*
here and that gave reason to an exquisite conservation
of the body, illogical though it seems to a modern
understanding, is a kind of privilege; moreover,
if a sacrifice comes into play, it is an artwork of
deification. We don't have to look any longer for such
causes as past experiences to account for the relation
between the different sensory phenomena, which
was erroneously termed synesthesia. It can't wait.
The boundary, which is internal and inextended and
which only connects, belongs to the level of infinity,
while the outer boundary or relation, which at the
same time connects and separates, belongs to the level
of space and matter, to the finite. Trees light. The
season was definitely over. That is desire disguised   *"Element"*
as pure desire and not itself, which is the desire that   *and element.*
springs from memory and which characterizes the
man of time. Whichever; I'm tired. Where is the
purpose in predicting? Every namable thing, act, or
relation has numerous properties, qualities or aspects.
In our minds the properties of each thing, together
with its name, form an associated group. If different
parts of the brain are severally concerned with the
several properties, and a farther part with the hearing,
and still another with the uttering, of the name, there
must inevitably be brought about such a dynamic
connection amongst all these brain-parts that the

activity of any one of them will be likely to spark the
activity of all the rest. A sprained ankle, a dislocated
arm, are in danger of being sprained or being
dislocated again; and if we ascend to the nervous
system, we find how many so-called functional
diseases seem to keep themselves going simply
because they happen to have once begun; and how
the forcible cutting short by medicine of a few attacks
is often sufficient to enable the physiological forces
to get possession of the field again, and to bring the
organs back to functions of health. So, I ask, again,
what is the point in predicting? The need to emerge
from oneself? To keep the flag flying? I don't know
how to write about it and won't even attempt to use
the purely incidental fact that I'm still living. Strange
men, and strange animals, either large or small, excite
fear, but especially men or animals advancing toward
us in a threatening way. Similarly, the rediscovery
of uncommon or singular apparatuses, novel and
fantastic as they might be, is neither decisive nor
fully adequate to formulate an inclusive approach
that distinguishes it from connoisseurship. In other
words—I am someone who knows the degree and
nature of guilt. And others are continually arriving.

That was a mistake. It would be better not to speak
here of function.

New people placed in old situations. The great epic
is built on the analysis of a mass movement. That is,
we do not care whether there be any real sameness in
things or not, or whether the mind be true or false in

its assumptions of it. The only question for us is as to
what the consciousness may mean when it calls the
present self the same with one of the past selves which
it has in mind. All a backdrop to escape. For escape.
I'll say this once more, in different words: Anna fell
under the train. What else is there? Something always
adheres, and a love which is no longer unconditional
is already in a precarious state. It's best to know
nothing about it. If it is true that these catastrophes
are the expression of a clash of the individuality of
the organism with the otherness of the world, then
the organism must proceed from catastrophe to
catastrophe. I hope that I may not be misunderstood.
The voice, becoming more distant.

The simplest thing is the most incredible thing, the
most incredible thing is the most remarkable thing,
which requires examination. The formalities of the
process were in themselves merely tactics for delay.

I was a young man who wanted what was good and
was training myself inwardly toward this end; any
honest person will understand that it made a bad
impression on me to hear, in minute detail, all these
anecdotes about negligence and omission. And yet
there's something calming and comforting about
them, too—like all things simple and necessary. If   *Further tensions.*
we assume that that every reaction is determined
by the nature or "essence" of the organism, if we
regard equalization as an equalization toward a
mean, adequate to the nature of the organism in a
given situation, then the question arises: What do we

mean by the term "nature"? For once a man loses his
connection with whatever looms forever larger than
himself, he has lost himself as well. He exists solely as
a nexus after that, a mere contingency, a crossroads
without a place name. He draws back. In the
weakness of the moment. He had devised a concrete
plan on how to live. He gave it different meanings.
And he would parade—flying over those roads
covered with snow. And that's the way he grieves. And
death whispers in his ear: "You are afraid of me." To
single out any one of these things from a total vastness
is partially to introduce order into the vastness.

Where are our dead friends? Is there any comfort?
The coloring crude, the design profoundly simplified.
It is no more true to say he locates that pain in
his body, than to say he locates his body in that
pain. Gone from me now was I myself, and all that
remained were the hard bright surfaces of a self that
generated no light but merely reflected back whatever
surfaces it met.

Through these instruments the interface emerged,
through these instruments a fragile imaginary was
brought to light, through these instruments time,
sound, and reflex, could be seen, through these
instruments the world was no longer a paltry given—
it was a moving target, a dynamic presence, it was,
to put it bluntly, alive. I had discerned the correct
relationships of the larger sections and the smallest
details of the rich but always appropriate decoration;
but now I also ascertained the reciprocal connections

between these manifold ornaments, the articulation of
one main part with the other, the interlacing of details
that are analogous but very divergent in form, ranging
from saint to monster, from leaf to spike. It can all
turn out fine. Taking a share in power is thus also
having one's voice heard. Help it. This is a subject that
can be started from any place, since all the important
connections in the linkages of circumstance must pass
through detail, and none of them are less important
than others. Everything depends on that. You are
walking toward gunshots on this road, while the
steppe is asking for songs.

But to do so cheerfully! A big tree with its own crown
and its own leaves. This is now an incorrect life of
my themes. But the future does exist. I can hardly
remember a more pleasant feeling: Here I was, sitting
again at this threshold, over which I had shortly
before stumbled out in despair.

The wheels roll over the beautiful woman. *Force from without.*

So, the fluctuation. Peculiarities of excitation. Any
new stimulus can still exist. All this shows that in the *The dance.*
reflex, so-called, we are dealing with a special type of
coming to terms of organism and environment. One
becomes more constant as the other is distended. The
reflex is the figure, while the activity of the rest of the
organism is the background.

The facts, however, call for another interpretation:
Everyone's dearest wish is to have useful things free
of charge.

A day of rain in the middle of June. An apology,
playgrounds. Birds in courtship, insects indicating
nectar.

This is how we've finally gotten back to the road that
we left in order to look at some of the surroundings,
the road that none of us can leave—we can never
leave it. Since a willed movement is a movement
preceded by an idea of itself, the problem of the
will's education is the problem of how the idea of a
movement can arouse the movement itself. This, as we
have seen, is a secondary kind of process; for framed
as we are, we can have no *a priori* idea of a movement,
no idea of a movement which we have not already
performed. Before the idea can be generated, the
movement must have occurred in a blind, unexpected
way, and left its idea behind.

I take pills to do this. Anyone who sets out to describe
the religious experience of an era whose fundamental   *False ways.*
experience is the absence of religious experience, even
if this absence also constitutes an experience, faces
a difficult task. If we try to factually describe it, we
have to transform it into an object like other objects
whereby its primal character of attitude, feeling,
and so on, is lost and distorted into a thing. This is
something to respect, I think, something to admire.
But what of describing the desire to experience a
religious experience in a body whose fundamental
experience is one of absence, of disbelief? One answer
replaces another. I hope that the reader will realize
that this digression into philosophical problems is

not determined by the casual, personal inclination
of the author but that the material itself imposes the
obligation on us. I would have broken every window
in the house. Work changes a person. I think I'm in
the position of a cyclist who can't ride on the road
because there are too many cars and can't ride on
the sidewalk because there are too many pedestrians.
After a certain amount of effort of attention has been
given to an idea, it is manifestly impossible to tell
whether either more or less of it might have been
given or not. To tell that, we should have to ascend
to the antecedents of the effort, and defining them
with mathematical exactitude, prove, by laws of
which we have not at present even an inkling, that the
only amount of sequent effort which could possibly
comport with them was the precise amount which
actually came. We are thrown back therefore upon
the crude evidences of introspection on the one hand,
with all its liabilities to deception, and, on the other
hand, upon a priori postulates and probabilities. The
more we put into the definition, the less certain we
are it exists. I'm talking about conscious visualization.
Complex perception, then, is connected with
scrutinizing, squinting, bulging one's eyes and almost
touching an object with them. Look at this. At least
animals with such disturbances do not simply perish.
What does it mean: "Saw fit"? Whenever such a thing
is met with by us now, out sagacity notes it to be of
a certain kind; our learning immediately recalls that
kind's kind, and then that kind's kind, and so on; so
that a moment's thinking may make us aware that the
thing is of a kind so remote that we could never have

directly perceived the connection. Though you are
seen, you cannot see, and though you are heard, you
cannot hear, and though others will walk along with
you, you may not walk along with them.

Projection oscillates between two extreme poles of
meaning: first, the spectacular proof—in the literal
sense of the expression—that something, which is
sent through an image machine, was or is like what
we see in the half-space of the screen; second, the
production of a reality as an image, which exists as we
see it only in the projection.

What we call sensation, in a special sense modality,
is but a very complicated special instance of a total
reaction pattern of the organism during its coming
to terms with those events of the environment that
demand sensory experience. I won't eat another fruit.
Long, dreadful minutes pass in silence. It is the fusion
of endurance and perspective.

Each act of conception results from our attention   *Outer boundaries.*
singling out some one part the world presents without
confusion. The mind may change its states, and its
meanings, at different times; may drop one, take
up another, but the dropped conception can in no
intelligible sense be said to change into its successor.

The spreading out bears relation to the growing point.

Anyone, provided he can be amusing, has the right   *Inner parallels.*
to talk to himself. By doing so he becomes a person
of his own times, a contemporary.

If someone who is accustomed to hold his head
somewhat obliquely is forced to hold it straight,
this is not only a special effort for him, but after
a certain time the head will return to the usual,
"normal" position, unless he prevents this by
continuously paying attention to his head. All the
observer sees is noise in relation to the code, a crisis
in relation to value. We see then that we are dealing
with fluctuating material. It is what welcomes and
rejects. He is an ordinary person. This is the distance
between meaning and verification. In the face of the   *Further tensions.*
arbitrary nature of the organic world, the line and
point become a locus of repose. His choice. There
and back.

Becoming is an unstable unrest which settles into
stable result. Experience is predicated on existence.
As is behavior.

Under such circumstances there could be no thought
of an intimate conversation relating only to ourselves.
There is no real substitution. Continuity can be arranged.
We have not moved ahead, not really. They are
shaking the so-called decorative walls. A thread tied
around the finger, an unusual constricting of the
clothing, will feel as if still there, long after they have
been removed. A large point of small points.

So much for the apparent shortening of tracts of time
in retrospect. This notion of the outer world building
up a sort of mental duplicate of itself if only we give
it time, is so easy and natural in its vagueness that one
hardly knows how to start to criticize it. Close your

eyes and simply wait to hear somebody tell you that a
minute has elapsed.

That's why they defend themselves so desperately.
Forced to choose between comment and cause.

4.

Autumn it gestures.

Hasn't us in after, tall grass on water.

Distant lit

scenes (a-

part, land-

scapes with-

out sound) re-

mind sight.

To move and the play.

There is no generally skeptical origin.
There is a film that can be watched purely as an abstract
examination of light and space, a simple fusion

we construct of our endurance, our simplest perspectives
exploited by maneuvers, rich depths felt by leeway in the ways
speech maps acts. It has, from above, a thin them; a view

which is stagnant. Two bodies script contrasting plays:
the slow dispersion of the substantive (in its concretion
via treatment, seeming kinship) versus photographic art

in relational equilibrium (the torture of it, plantlike
indifference). One could call it drawing in two voices
only one of which admits that that empathic hand

has its own will and will, in gesture, say so. It's the same
argument: beliefs, at the time of retrieval, lead to intersticed
togetherness. Allegiance debility—how it is our distant

residence. In prerequisites for motion, nothing violates
our assumptions of normality, linearity, or even
loveliness in variance. Our interiority decomposes

in deference to itself. When togetherness, inside the given
codes of inclusion and representation refelt, collapses
as an activity that is an end in itself, it creates another

code of gross familiarity—we speak and plan the planning of
the utterance while speaking. Mediumistic landscapes
architecture the supposedly reminded at. Scenery:

that part of anything anything won't relinquish. Setting:
the way we able misremembered houses, whole worlds
ideal relation recognizes as supposed to, should have. Why not

take me to a concert. Why not secret our concerns
about conviction, its tall, elastic figure. Call it our detachment
misunreadiness, our impulse as impulsion, inactive vacillation

in the midst of which I call myself a sudden interruption.
Call myself the agent of the first-followed arc in the gradual
unfolding of a simple work. Then a second will reveal itself:

to move and the play; the object which it isolates.
The lightness (or its opposite) of reciprocation rests
only if we dampen our own amplitude. Combined

inside that sequence, refusing us together, is knowledge,
its circulation, its reinvention as commitment to the one thing
aloneness can accomplish: an acceptance of discovery

as the finding of a something that was already there.
That there is a difference, then, in thinking and believing
without the body, even if the body is just the vocalized

part of our particular day-to-day which enables in us
slow and strengthless growth coming into being as the means
to make one so dear to us disabled, saying: nothing

can be done. I am calling out the name that I don't know.
I am standing on the body that I see before I dress—
there are two and both pretend—appalled, as if to say

fuck, yes, rain, drown the sick one, either or. I want to watch
stiff limbs purposed in the current, his mass in two halves
gash pale and ungainly as I wave (again, again, it's me

this time) the happy capsize of a will-less frame.
But I'm a dad now. See? There is only ever one
trajectory. All we do is choose the vessel

which can't be true. A pairing is a pivot and a fall
made constant by another's sick volition. Experience insists
that division destroy the character. And yet there is the call

we mention, the ringing not called call but we call name.
Two can occupy the objects factionally various
even if they are reflections. The questioning of origin

doesn't really question origin, it eliminates the skepticism
wherefrom with its feeling. No words. Not yet.
Always in a picture. The line by swinging back and forth

becomes a pendulum. But I know that that is only one
way of knowing all our different things at once. And the whole,
when the whole moves, it pretends toward resentment.

To do in order not to do it gone.

    and, against detachment, trying

(lightnessed and am let aside)

    without.

Given in at

all, off

Proportion is a correspondence among the measures

and tends to be before appearing
automatic, each of these abnormal

centers, mechanistic. Proper speaking
let it call it his is her vestibular

cell; what in want lights either
compound thing sustaining parts

absolutely insulated. If he gives then
from her, of him, irreducible

pluralism two with feeling
so convey: in addition, from a sympathy

descending, finely, pliable, one
disorder under answer with an eye

for cause abandons. A company
intermediate, it performs it for itself

the lack of adequate reproduction
theory poses higher problems:

presentational circularity
between the poles. Incommunicable

distance, vast mimetic rejections.
Correlated motions, similarly

predetermined, name in numbers
probability eloquences. Surface

exaggeration, disproportion, formal
excitation—designed to center

temporality—actively prohibits
the advancement of the gestural.

Where within the body, intersective
absence is the only strict example

as his in her, each of these, wants
twice felt, one mind. Breath gives

breath by answer one disorder
which it cuts, compound parts

descending justly yet again
denied divides. Contained relations

feeling other. Felt disorder
wanting, felt enumeration gives it

absolutely her and with him.
Wherein is the body. Secondary

sympathy, where and when the eye
falls. What takes the hand

the hand memorial, is a treatment
where disease itself performs him

connection between the origins—
perfection, assemblage—is the first

among prerequisites for affective
analogous function. At rest

in the middle of everything is
the sun; the work of true proximity

animation; an ordinary resilience.
Courses through causes, painful

reductions of retributory greenness
held a center and circumference

once elsewhere, now elsewhere.
Retouching something spoken

first among convergence
follows waking, tangents, behaving

has him lit or her in light together.
Passive. Found among the causes

same as any other. That air indifferent
answered last a positively

joined disorder with abandon
absolutely, plied relationed excess

from the victim since redacted, sent
a different lit solution, proved

what in where diseased in treatment.
Twice the body twice enacted.

In her, him with other; with him
her within it. Disease increased

beside its sympathy: splitting each
a presence, companioning in illness.

(an antecostuming

passage, called

          a coalescence   )

On I say on I go.

                                        Day the same I forgive you
            everything and there is

                                        nothing to forgive.

                                        A light we call pause.
                                        A strong light like sunlight.

                                        Where were we
                                        when in

wires without

                                        hands if not for portraiture.

(

if then

this, then

conscience by

)

Not just temporal distance, but history.

You are my rest of my departmentalized
mind, a means, an accidental

conscience without hope, magnanimity
without cause: all the minor non-accidents

secreted for the approval of our
perceived-to-be betters. As if no one

combed the landscape's hair; the view, in it
value, manifests itself as individual

decomposition in the unwatchful
trust of shared lives: is it necessary, do I

have to, help me see it, do not knock—
the violence done forgets the violence did.

The only responsible course is to deny
the means, the cause, the cordoning of how

nice of you, believe me, the equally trying
safety of, of / you are my rest of my

familiar indifference, a movement's
hesitation, deliberation. No one escapes

this entertainment. The two consolidated
gardens of pre-condition are both called

background, they appear on a
questionnaire, measured by the principle

that all this is no more a formalistic
administrative way of settling the frigid

aloofness of loved ones, the unwatchful
trust of isolation made worse

by agreement, the recent, almost / you are
my rest of my model of the unhappy

capacity, immediate impossibility,
the quality, in it value, a reversal seems near—

within it, earlier pain, then here pain—
the objection that all this is no more

an overbearing matter-of-factness
between delight in emptiness and the lie

on the one hand, on the other, occultism
is a symptom of regression. The realm

of reification and standardization is thus
(with a few isolated and hypostasized

categories) thought, allowing itself to be
reminded that nobody believes anybody.

You are my rest of my apologia
of perversion, that, that kind, that kind of

how every undistorted friendship is a gift
that people who belong together

stay apart for. This principle, positivistic,
within it, without which, those who feel

an equal revulsion for pleasure, meaning
conscience, magnanimity, inappropriate

isolation, worse by agreement, relational
indifference, no matter how familiar

the object which it isolates—I have forgotten
to save in my object something of the calm

manifesting itself as consolidated
gardens of principle, positivistic, without

which, within it you / you are my rest of my
long, contemplative look. Really, look.

It does not take a form. In a pure looking-on
you are no longer really looked at.

One need only have once heard the deeper
divergence of an opposition. One need

only have once heard the objection
that all this is no more even hearable

as appearance, measured by principle.
Capacity notwithstanding, the rest

is the idea that, despite what we recognize,
the recent past presents itself destroyed.

5.
Twentieth century.

This history recorded is the history
of area and how expression poses
problems for us. I bought her her dress
myself. Speculative

                          romances, filiation
substantially maligned, we were met
with aberration, frames too vast, graphists
verbal and pictorial

                          halved unmitigated
loneliness. This boy is dead and yesterday
topology. Scholastic treatises exhibited
nearly everything

           we ever knew and still
the crops in yard went green to white
and not the better white, neither auspice,
the one instead that weights

                          at fulfill the plans
for milk and meat. At first there was no
disbelief, actual evacuation. The sudden
upped in temperature

                       burst to fume and all
talked wedding, quick, tension and credit
gathering aerial information, picked
a base and went

                                   "why aren't you laughing"
when they didn't really mean it. Heliotropes
like foam, butlery in film then. Petersburg
even more touched

                          than before. Then again
was she sure she didn't want to leave. Cleaning
up the seasonal, the datum at the place of it—if
it, if we stopped

                          it, it could only—then
yes, a summer home. Quadrant out the views
before the views go while. At their amplest there
were thousands building

                              tundra railways so that
everywhere transports vehicles closer together.
One drive, one drives. A good man sells
a gray painting. How much

                              could it cost to make
rooms cooler than at outside? The hour's present
time and hour pass and hour both the futures
know behind the branch

                              that objectivity meets
the lower part of transit. Discontinuation
between the poles. A canal and a canal despite
concurrence, cross each

                          other, one the sluice
above the channel. She hired theorization
groups upwards of insurance fraud
for twice the original

                          medicine out; computation
backwards from herselves. What friend is
is lime scent where figure varnish can
distract it, longways

                          enacts the hand to vanish
what had once it held it every. August
summarily, better off, resentment for
admission costs to caverns

                        stalactitic franchise.
Concern for accrediting bodies, methods
for total encompassment—parental guile
to gatecrashing—drift

                        into more films about
silence and touchy subjects designed
to overcome the worrisome affinity
for commercial traveling

                        maxims. They ceased
devaluing younger siblings—the reflex
determined original in individuals
inviolately scattered out

                        at a time when the basis
of the right is in itself defiling the final
hiding places of instinctual drives. Get on
up there. Add a little

                        of that jittery hand
business with the fingers held apart. Say it
with me, deprivation purification. Removal
resolution. Who would

                        say were it weren't, how
to play when it burn. Vaguely negative
values, capability resolutely, decisions
malformed able habits

                              that it clear the aptest
fences. I am again no more a father
than a mother. Do not remember feeling
now is then. Lost. Broad

                              origin, broad origin.
We minimized the variables most prone
to confound. We knew the average pitch
of voice; what was was

                              what had half. There
must be someone due involved in vacancy.
The place it will be, that it accepts to be,
is for which we drain

                    the swimming pool.
Undesiring motion is not a motion inside
but a thanks for our seizures in the shape of
limits, and a blanket

                        to disorient us comfortably
up the stair step. Temptation is noisy
where the dust moves even all. I appreciate
your calling as you did despite my silence.

The title *One day you finish to be a boy* is from Kurt Schwitters.

The titles "The protogenesis of form is a character of compromise" and "The eye travels paths cut out for it in work" are from Paul Klee.

The title "Proportion is a correspondence among the measures" is from Vitruvius.

The title "That virtues acquired by death have a retroactive effect" is from Ambrose Bierce.

The title "And, not content with circumscription, spreads" is from John Singleton.

Portions of *Conversation in black laughs; Or, This is the way we ride the bike* recast texts by E.M. Cioran, Thomas Eakins, and William James. The text's subtitle, *This is the way we ride the bike*, is from Mathilda Hummel.

Point and Line to Plane is a work of collage. The utilized texts, page-numbers therein, order of deployment, number of occurrences of original sentences by the author, and the sequence of intertitles were determined by the use of a random integer generator (www.random.org/integers). The title of the work, as well as its intertitles, are from Wassily Kandinsky's book of the same name.

Attali, Jacques. *Noise: The Political Economy of Music.* Trans. Brian Massumi. Minneapolis: U of Minnesota P, 1985.

Banks, Russell. *The Relation of My Imprisonment.* New York: HarperCollins, 1996.

Baudelaire, Charles. *The Intimate Journals of Charles Baudelaire.* Trans. Christopher Isherwood. Boston: Beacon Press, 1957.

Flaubert, Gustave. *The Temptation of Saint Anthony.* Trans. Lafcadio Hearn. New York: Random House, 2001.

Goethe, Johann Wolfgand von. *From My Life: Poetry and Truth (Parts One to Three).* Ed. Thomas P. Saine and Jeffrey L. Simmons. Trans. Robert R. Heitner. Princeton: Princeton UP, 1994.

Goldstein, Kurt. *The Organism: A Holistic Approach to Biology Derived from Pathological Data in Man.* New York: Zone Books, 1995.

James, William. *The Principles of Psychology*. New York: Dover, 1950.

Kandinsky, Wassily. *Point and Line to Plane*. Trans. Howard Dearstyne and Hilla Rebay. New York: Dover, 1979.

Mann, Thomas. *Buddenbrooks: The Decline of a Family*. Trans. John E. Woods. New York: Knopf, 1994.

Shklovsky, Viktor. *Energy of Delusion: A Book on Plot*. Trans. Shushan Avagyan. Champaign: Dalkey Archive, 2007.

Silliman, Ron. *The Age of Huts (compleat)*. Berkeley: U of California P, 2007.

Zielinski, Siegfried and Silvia M. Wagnermaier, eds. *Variantology I: On Deep Time Relations of Arts, Sciences, and Technologies*. Köln: Verlag der Buchhandlung Walther König, 2005.

The poem "On I say on I go" is dedicated to Kathleen Brian.

The refrain "You are my rest of my…" in "Not just temporal distance, but history" is from the line "You are my rest of my life to wear space into" by Christopher Knowles.

Acknowledgements.

Grateful acknowledgements to the editors of the following journals where versions of these poems first appeared: *Boston Review*: To move and the play; *Colorado Review*: Proportion is a correspondence among the measures (I); *Gulf Coast*: Not just temporal distance, but history; *JERRY*: The eye travels paths cut out for it in work; *Modern Review*: A distance of psychosomatic recall, On I say, on I go, Proportion is a correspondence among the measures (II), Twentieth Century; *Oversound Poetry:* The protogenesis of form is a character of compromise, That virtues acquired by death have a retroactive effect, Once when hours, once when it is over, Hasn't us in after, tall grass on water; *A Public Space*: And, not content with circumscription, spreads.

Special thanks to the editors of Projective Industries and Cannibal Books for publishing portions of this manuscript in the chapbooks *Point and Line to Plane* and *Autumn it gestures*.

Many thanks also to the teachers, colleagues, editors, and friends with whom I have had the privilege of sharing time and mind, formal and otherwise: Stephanie Anderson, Mary Jo Bang, Sommer Browning, Lucie Brock-Broido, Dan Chelotti, Syl Cheney-Coker, Alexandra Crosier, Todd Steele Grogan, Matt Henriksen, Robert M. Johanson, Brett Fletcher Lauer, Tony Mancus, Glyn Maxwell, Rusty Morrison, Ethan Paquin, Andrew Seguin, Jesse Seldess, Anne Tardos, and Mark Valadez.

For finding something of value herein, heartfelt gratitude and admiration are due to Julie Carr. And for their tireless efforts bringing this book into the world, to Noah Eli Gordon, HR Hegnauer, and everyone at Subito Press: thank you for your extraordinary work.

And, finally, I am endlessly indebted to: my parents, for their support; Richard Howard, for his unerring discernment; Timothy Donnelly, for his inexplicable precision; Robert Ostrom, for is heart; Samuel Amadon, for his permanence; Mathilda Hummel, for always and everything and anywhere and us; and Kathleen Brian, for a life on two continents.

Subito Press Titles.

2008

Little Red Riding Hood Missed the Bus by Kristin Abraham

With One's Own Eyes: Sherwood Anderson's Realities
by Sherwood Anderson
Edited and with an Introduction by Welford D. Taylor

My Untimely Death by Adam Peterson

Dear Professor, Do You Live in a Vacuum? by Nin Andrews

2009

Self-Titled Debut by Andrew Farkas

F-Stein by L.J. Moore

2010

Song & Glass by Stan Mir

Moon Is Cotton & She Laugh All Night by Tracy Debrincat

Bartleby, the Sportscaster by Ted Pelton

2011

The Body, The Rooms by Andy Frazee

Death-in-a-Box by Alta Ifland

Man Years by Sandra Doller

2012

We Have With Us Your Sky by Melanie Hubbard

Vs. Death Noises by Marcus Pactor

The Explosions by Mathias Svalina

2013

Because I Am the Sea I Want to Be the Shore by Renée Ashley

The Cucumber King of Kėdainiai by Wendell Mayo

Domestic Disturbances by Peter Grandbois

2014

Liner Notes by James Brubaker

As We Know by Amaranth Borsuk & Andy Finch

Letters & Buildings by Thomas Hummel

About Subito Press.

Subito Press is a non-profit literary publisher based in the Creative Writing Program of the Department of English at the University of Colorado at Boulder. Subito Press encourages and supports work that challenges already-accepted literary modes and devices.

Subito Press.

Noah Eli Gordon, *director*
Adrian Sobol, *managing editor*
Alexis Almeida
Alexis Renee Smith
Connor Fisher
Lily Duffy
Liz McGehee
Sarena Ulibarri